Rise
of the
Dark Goddess

A COLLECTION OF POETRY

Rise of the Dark Goddess

A COLLECTION OF POETRY

CASSANDRA L. THOMPSON

QUILL & CROW PUBLISHING HOUSE

Rise of the Dark Goddess by Cassandra L. Thompson
Published by Quill & Crow Publishing House

Designed by Lauren Hellekson

Printed in the United States of America.

ISBN 978-1-7356863-3-2

Author's Website: http://cassandralthompson.carrd.co

For
The Writing Community

I heard her call long ago,
She of blood and bone and crow,
as I scoured the woods in a child's body,
two wolves keeping vigil
as I knelt in the creek to pray.

She was still
until they abused me,
and she gently unfolded her wings,
warning false prophets,
"Back off, she's one of mine."

She laid in wait as the rage consumed me,
swallowing my violence,
until I turned it on myself.
She howled in those moments,
She of warriors and wolves,
waiting for her daughter to come home.

In severed locks and afterbirth
she finally emerged,
she of victory and death,
turning my words into hers,
sending me her crows,
wondering
if I was ready at last
to heed
the raven's call.

Sunset twisting through barren trees
Raped by the wind of their colorful leaves
This is the place you will find me
Transcendent of all that seeks to bind me
Parched leaves swirling about the floor
Whispers of dead magic and forgotten lore
Mouths cry out, attempt to possess
Falling for the ruse of the kind seductress
But I am the barren womb, the mistress of lies
Harbinger of all you despise
The mother of crows, the destructor of dreams,
The tumultuous roar of a dozen streams.
Come to the gates if you must, but a warning to those who leer,
Abandon all hope, ye who enter here.

She lingers
in cemeteries
longing
for a death
she cannot have
dreaming dreams
of rotting memories
a beautiful face
that hides away
the slow torment
of immortality.

I was thinking
of the lie
that happy endings exist,
wondering
if we can
jump past it
to the part where we
creak and ache,
remnants ready
to embrace
the lingering darkness,
hand in hand,
hoping
it will be shattered
by mercy.

Ours is a
relationship
closer than old friends,
he greets me like a lost lover
wrapping me up in arms
of dread and sorrow,
a suffocating embrace
that squeezes my heart
and lies heavy on my chest,
the despair warm,
the melancholy familiar,
with me as I sit
listless and blank
waiting for the day
he decides to abandon me.

Severed veins
spill words onto the page,
summoning dark gods
and ancient lovers,
Creatrix spinning worlds,
weaving threads of Universe
until she shrivels and dies,
waiting to rise again.

He carves stories into my skin,
burning for me
while I bleed for him,
our ritual
as we lie
under a blanket of stars,
limbs splayed out
on a bed of ash and bone.

We lie beneath twisted branches
entwined in the fallen leaves
I tell you I want to rest here,
to one day become the tree.
Before you can reply,
I know you want to be tossed
into the sea.
You smile sadly,
wishing I was your queen.
I remind you gently,
that all we see or seem
is but a dream within a dream.

How I wish I could take you with me
Hand in hand as we explore every dream
But I have seen things you will never see
My eyes tell stories of things yet to be
Your youth deserves one less ancient than me
Your heart should have land, sky, mountain, and sea
My world is decay, death, and misery
To suffer deep is to fall in love with me.

Swirling through
Stygian waves
of irresolution,
she finds solace
in the howling of hounds,
the twisting of snakes,
and the rustle of
autumn leaves
scattered across
the cemetery floor.

Restless
Unsatisfied
Longing for things I cannot name.
Finding solace in impossible things,
hopeless dreams,
hollow words.
Distant fantasies
of what was meant to be,
aching for this curse
to be broken.

॰ᕲ

I exist
somewhere between
spiced lips
and the empty hands
of lonesome trees,
cradling
the sapphire sky.

Do not fall for me,
for there is nothing about me
that is like the rest,
I'll walk through flames to save you
but I'll stiffen in your embrace.

Do not fall for me,
for there is nothing about me
that is soft,
kissing me is broken glass
I find comfort in the shadows

Do not fall for me
for there is nothing about me
that is warm,
my hips may be seductive,
but my heart no longer beats.

A hundred souls
I've tried to capture
some survived,
I stayed broken.
Trapped in an eternal
fruitless search
that makes me wonder
why I ache
for the things
that are not mine.

Acrimonious
she exists
in a box of her own mind
never satisfied
no matter the surroundings,
rusted tears
to match an
iron clad heart
ruthlessly
forged out of flame
rancorous
until the bitter,
insurmountable
end.

I need more of you
Your flesh, under my nails
Your mouth, snake bite
Fill me with dying moth wings
Twist me up like one of your dolls
Tempt me, inspire me
Give me it all.

One day,
she hung up her skeletal wings
surrendering to the allure
of vapid exchange
until she found him
in the corner of her room
begging to be let free
outside,
but she couldn't
she wouldn't
her heart was a cage.

Ice Queen
sits on her throne of bones
untouchable,
hoping for a fool
to stumble over her roots
and prick his skin
on her thorns,
drops of blood
allowing her to feel,
making her feel
anything
anything
at all.

Tear open my back
To find my wings
Crown me with thorns
To see if I scream
Imprisoned by flesh
Branks-silenced
and scorned
It bears nothing
compared to
the love that I mourn.

I searched for him in the eyes of broken men,
my hands coming back empty,
Until the day he found me,
Whispered to me his secrets as he vanquished my enemies,
and we toasted their skulls in victory.
He loved me until I could love myself,
worship at my feet,
Lifting me up on crow feather wings,
And placing me on a throne,
Built of bones and ash.
I can still taste him on my lips,
My tongue burnt from his,
His claws still in my heart,
As I wait,
Longing,
Burning,
Until the day of my last breath,
And he comes to take me home.

Pinned wings
Taxidermy eyes
Entrail-painted floor
He steps back in admiration,
smiles,
as he tells me
I'm beautiful,
inside and out.

༄

I tried to lift you into the light,
but I pushed you into the sun.
I cried as you burst into flame.
I cradle your charred remains in my arms,
cursing myself for not warning you
that everything I touch
turns to ash.

He wanted a good girl
who obeyed men
and went to church.
So I wore a rosary
while I crucified him
and took my pound of flesh.

Always,
he promised,
as he slipped from my fingers.
I couldn't even cry
as he turned to dust.
I knew the day would come
for all things wither and die,
And can you ever truly
possess a ghost?

Little warrior
Grows up quick
Sharp
Fierce
Bright
Attracting those
Who want to snuff her out
Warm themselves by her fire
Use her to light their own flames.
Now warrior
Wanes weary
Seasoned
Strong
Hard
Burning brighter than ever
Tired
But unable
To ever
Give up the fight.

I keep him locked in my attic
until I cave,
letting him nibble my flesh
until he bites off my fingertips,
then I put him back up
until I can't resist him again.

He called me fake,
accused me of wearing a mask.
I showed him he was wrong,
peeling away my face
with a pocket knife.

She is
Eve's apple
Prometheus's ripped torso
Loki's poisoned flesh.
He is
Lucifer's revenge
Jesus's bloody thorns
Arachne's twisted legs.
She keeps his heart in a box made of skin,
He keeps a jar of her eyes.

I look for him
in the spaces between
clinking wind chimes
and the roar of waves.
He slips his fingers between
the translucent folds
of my dreamland
with me
during each
shuddering release
the subtle rise of hair along my skin
the calm breath after the storm
he created.

Blood trickles out of me
Leaky faucet drops
to the floor.
I lie still as
he reads my scars
like Braille
with his fingertips
and tongue.
I'm not alive,
but he won't let me die,
keeping me safe
lest I have to face
the darkness alone.

Bleed for me
Whisper me lies
Split your tongue
To lick my thighs
My body a tower
Poised to maim and maul
You must pay in full
To scale this wall.

I've memorized the slope
of your hands
the creases in your skin
as you spread my fingers apart
with yours,
drenched and breathless,
as we float
somewhere
between life and death,
like driftwood pulled in
by the sea.

In the still
eerie silence
of the first snowfall,
she waits,
buried beneath
the blanket of white,
pinned between here
and there
frozen
by indecision
trapped
at the crossroads.

His eyes linger over my lips,
tracing them with his thumb,
tells me they would look lovely
in a shade of pink,
smiles as he shows me
his collection
of petrified lips,
a gruesome collage
of rainbow kisses.

Manic,
cracked lips,
and bitten fingers,
I snag on the door,
my insides splattering the floor.
He sighs, puts down his paper and pieces me back together.
"You need to write," he reminds me, retrieving a chunk of my heart.
"But I'm keeping this for later."

Bleed for me,
she commanded,
pulling off her crown of thorns
and placing it
firmly
upon his head.

Rusted twine
holds together
parchment flesh
and tired bones.
You can have her
if your fingers can
unravel the slippery cords,
and pack back in
her warm insides before
she dismantles,
Sew her back together,
perhaps with ribbon,
so they don't notice she's broken.

Unlovable
degenerate
shattered
souls,
twin flames
trapped
in endless torment,
a lachrymose tale
of eternal separation.

She leapt from the towers of a heavenly realm
that could not hold her,
cradled by the earth as it filled in
her broken pieces,
the crows keeping vigil
as they waited
for their queen to rise.

❧

When he sleeps,
I take his hair,
weaving strands into spiderwebs,
hoping to catch him
when he dreams
and take him into my nightmares.

There is a girl
where my eyes should be
wound in gossamer threads
whispering frantic stories
of what was
and what shall never be
trapped
in a place
she can't breathe.

꙳

Surrounded by the dead,
I wondered if a woman outlives her husband,
and marries again,
if she is buried with husband the first,
or the second.
He pauses
thoughtfully,
and peers at me with
slate blue Scorpio eyes
and says, don't marry again.
He wants to be buried with me.

Enmeshed
Embedded in my skin
He is
A part of me
I can no longer tell
Where I end
And where he begins
Entangled
In the arms
of my reaper.

The air was biting cold as I held you,
a wraith of vapor escaping
from your parted lips
as you died,
taking your soul
along with it.

I pushed away
but he pushed harder
November's chill
seducing September's sunshine,
Vows between the cemetery stones
understanding that crows must fly free
but keeping a watchful eye
until I return.

I am an aching pile of
contorted limbs,
bewildered,
numb,
defenseless.
I have no energy for words,
but he answers,
"Good. Let's keep it that way."

Suspended
Disjointed
Mouth sewn shut
He pops out one of my eyes.
His favorite doll.

Chest to chest
Astride him
Breath hot in my ear
Finger tangled hair
I can smell him
Taste him
Touch him
But only for a moment
Before he crumbles
Into dust
And I'm reminded
once more
what it means to be
in love
with a ghost.

He rides each wave
determined to
see what is
deep
underneath
fighting as they rise
threatening to
swallow him
before he
can swallow me.

After three days
with knives in my back,
I realized
my crows had stilled.
I rose,
hobbling between raindrops,
hoping they'd see the food.
One called
before I could return,
a flurry of inky obsidian feathers
descending around me.
Black eyes
confirmed
that even when quiet,
they are there
always
with their mother.

Screaming
without a voice,
blinded,
I shiver as
rusted nails
drag across my skin.
I am lost,
trapped by shadow
as he whispers,
I am his,
safe now,
in his basement.

Her heart pours melancholia
chokes on sorrows
A poignant gift
most don't understand
He does,
washes away
her tears
with his blood.
They carve and weave
oceans and hellscapes,
bends in the forest
that bring them together
as they exist
and lament
over the
sunder of their
souls.

෴

Cozy and warm,
the scent of earth and fresh pine
in my nose
still dark as I open my eyes.
I am content,
peaceful even.
Until the horrible moment
I realize
I am buried alive.

I am lost,
swirling in October fog
dead leaves in the wind
reaching for out for anything
to ground me.

One by one
he pulled out my pins
until I unraveled,
a heap of skin
and bone
and hair
grateful for the release,
reminded
that nothing is forced,
that everything just is
and only his fingers
will do.

My love is a steady,
grounding presence,
near me always.
His voice,
baritone rumblings in my ear.
At night, he pulls me
close to his chest,
but I cannot turn to look.
I loathe to see his broken neck
still twisted from the hanging.

Cut out my heart for you
bleeding out on the bathroom floor
Shards of glass in my skin
where your hands should be
Eyes on the empty space beside me
the place where you should be.

After wandering
for a year
in unknown forests,
he finds her
split in two
brushes the dirt from her skin
lifts weeds from her hair
reminds her,
as he puts her halves back together,
that they are better than
status quo,
and it's a waste of time
pretending
they are.

Stop thinking
that there is any way
that earth could exist
without her sea.

I look for him
in the spaces between
clinking wind chimes
and the roar of waves.
He slips his fingers between
the translucent folds
of my dreamland
with me
during each
shuddering release
the subtle rise of hair along my skin
the calm breath after the storm
he created.

The air was biting cold as I held you,
a wraith of vapor escaping
from your parted lips
as you died,
taking your soul along with it.

I watch the dirt darken below me
drop
by
drop
streaming down by fingers,
oozing down the posts.
The vulture waits patiently nearby.
My only hope is that it picks me clean
after I have died,
my body collapsing
around the iron spikes of the gate.

He recites my poem:
"Someday
I will stop
enticing men
who drown me",
scribbles on the page,
replaces *entice* with *ignite*,
explaining I am his
harbinger of fire,
that he turns my flames
to ash
when his tide rises,
carrying the cinders
deep into him.

From deep in the mire of torment,
I rose,
spilling entrails onto the earth
as I walked
skin snagging on rocks
until my skeleton
reached the end
only to look up
and find someone
as dead as me.

She walks
a path of thorns
dying roses in her hair,
black lace sweeping
snake-bitten lips.
She rides
tormented waves
of suffering,
believing lies
that the end
will never come.

Discover more from this author at
www.quillandcrowpublishinghouse.com